Eat, Drink, and Be Merry!

Eat, Drink, and Be Merry!

RONALD C. STARENKO

CONCORDIA PUBLISHING HOUSE
ST. LOUIS   LONDON

Concordia Publishing House, St. Louis, Missouri
Concordia Publishing House Ltd., London, E. C. 1
Copyright © 1971 Concordia Publishing House
Library of Congress Catalog Card No. 72-157383
ISBN 0-570-03123-0

Contents

48260

Introduction

The tunes and lyrics of rock music, as well as the new liturgical forms of the church, invite people to share in the joyfulness of living. The popular trend today, secular or sacred, is the celebration of life.

Despite the pathos and tragedy of human existence people want to believe that life is worth living. We fight against war and poverty and disease, because we realize that unless we are able to enjoy life — the warmth of love and friendship, the freedom of the human spirit, self-expression in the arts — we have lost the logic of living. Even the use of mind- and life-expanding drugs represents the desperate search for a transcendent experience of enjoyment.

It is a mistake to lump together all human seeking of enjoyment under the philosophy of pleasure. Not all celebration, even the worldly variety, is immoral. Hedonism has been around a long time and people have always resorted to multiplying forms of escape, but there are honest and responsible attempts among people everywhere to find something in life worth celebrating.

Much merrymaking today is a reaction to the stance that the church took in medieval times toward the enjoyment of the body. And not a few Christians since have regarded the joys of the "spirit" as the only commendable ones.

Still, whatever distortions the Christian faith has suffered at the hands of those who could not quite enjoy life in the body, Christians today are seeking to recover the celebration character of human existence. What they affirm is nothing other than the Christian Gospel.

Christians are people who choose to celebrate the joy they have found in God, and they do not propose to do it by renouncing life on this earth or by repudiating the functions of the human body. On the contrary, they believe that if God enjoyed what He had made, and if it is a joy for Him to recover what was lost, then we have a reason to celebrate.

When Christ left His church the Sacrament of His Supper, He gave us the means to celebrate. We do not have to live in another world or get out of the body in order to affirm the reality of God's grace. We are privileged rather to participate in the fellowship of a meal that is already, as Martin Luther reminded us, "life and salvation." The forgiveness of sins is the freedom to receive God and rejoice in His presence, to renew our union with Him and all things.

In these chapters we have no illusions of presenting anything new, but we do have a vision of a life style that has at times lost some of its zing. In so doing we are not setting the posture of celebration against other Christian attitudes, such as contrition and confession. As a matter of fact, we would contend that contrition and confession can be healthy expressions of the Christian's relationship to God and to other people precisely because under the Gospel of forgiveness we are able to love God and our brother. The dominant note therefore for the living of our lives is promise and hope and joy.

The only appropriate response is celebration.

Eat, Drink, Be Merry!

Perhaps the toast — and the title of this book — to eat, drink, and be merry has always reminded us of a pagan and sensual philosophy of life, nothing at all what a Christian should embrace. In reference to this style of living our Lord tells a story (Luke 12:15-20) about a man who made good in business, so good that he has to start thinking about expansion. According to the story the man makes his plans to put away a fortune in order to take it easy — to eat, drink, and be merry. And Jesus calls him a fool, because that night his soul would be required of him.

What was the man's sin? That he wanted to take it easy, that he liked to eat, drink, and be merry? Hardly. There is no indication that his goods were ill-gotten, that he was unlucky to be so fortunate, that he did wrong in wanting to enjoy leisure or retirement.

That's not our problem either. As a matter of fact, our problem, like that of the man in the story, could very well be that we can't take it easy, that we have difficulty eating, drinking, and being merry. So feverish our activity becomes sometimes that we cannot even begin to enjoy life. Working long hours, getting in overtime, coming home dead-tired, we often find it impossible to celebrate.

Certainly our trouble is not that we want to enjoy life. How we wish we could! Even though it may appear that Jesus is warning us against the pleasures of this life in the story of the rich fool, the Biblical admonition is mostly positive. The Preacher of the Old Testament reminds us that "there is nothing better for them [men] than to be happy and enjoy themselves as long as they live; also that it is God's gift to man that everyone should eat and drink and take pleasure in all his toil. . . . There is nothing better than that a man should enjoy his work" (Ecclesiastes 3:12-13, 22). In a later chapter he writes:

> Go, eat your bread with enjoyment, and drink your wine with a merry heart. . . . Enjoy your life with the wife whom you love, all the days of your vain life . . . because that is your portion in life and in your toil. . . . Whatever your hand finds to do, do it with your might; for there is no work or thought or knowledge or wisdom in Sheol, to which you are going. (9:7-10)

"Eat, drink, and be merry, for tomorrow we die." Is there something to that ancient philosophy after all? If God intended life to be enjoyment, why do we often fail to achieve it? What accounts for our anxiety? The rich man in the story was no fool because he wanted to enjoy life. His trouble was that he didn't seek it in the right place. Our Lord introduced that little parable with the words: "Take heed, and beware of all covetousness; for a man's life does not consist in the abundance of his possessions." The rich fool, however, believed that his life had meaning, that his future was secure, if he had ample goods. Then, he thought, he could eat, drink, and be merry.

But that was his folly: he centered his life on goods instead of God. What is it that deprives us of enjoyment of life? That we have all too few possessions? That we don't have job security? That the future is always uncertain? That we might not live long enough to enjoy what we have accumulated? That today our soul might be required of us? No, it is not these possibilities that ruin our joy. It is rather, as Jesus tells us, the misfortune of not being "rich toward God."

There is a hymn that makes the point rather well:

> All depends on our possessing
> God's abundant grace and blessing,

Tho' all earthly wealth depart.
He who trusts with faith unshaken
In his God is not forsaken
And e'er keeps a dauntless heart.

He who hitherto hath fed me
And to many joys hath led me,
Is and ever shall be mine.
He who did so gently school me,
He who still doth guide and rule me,
Will remain my help divine.

Yes, "all depends on our possessing God's abundant grace and blessing." It is not our goods that put joy into life; it is the goodness of God! That is what Jesus is teaching in the story of the rich fool: a man's life consists in the abundance of God's goodness.

Our Lord was not one who was against eating and drinking and being merry. Instead, that is what He came to restore to men. Why, as a matter of fact, He was accused of being a "winebibber" because He did not adopt the rather strict ways of John the Baptist. And He was repeatedly criticized for eating and drinking with sinners. It was clear to people that Jesus believed that life should be enjoyed, that man should be able to celebrate God and rejoice in all His gifts.

To restore us to joy, our Lord understood, 12 involved more than helping words and healing works. It was His cross at last that made it possible for us to eat, drink, and be merry. When all things appeared to be vanity, as the author of Ecclesiastes observed, God sent His Son into the world. Through Jesus' seemingly futile struggle against the Evil One He conquered sin and death. When we are full of anxiety and lacking in trust toward God, God shows His concern for us in the death of Jesus. When we are weak and weary, the victims of greed, He comes to be with us and to feed us the Bread of Life. God wants us to have peace, to be able to let go, to give up striving long enough to enjoy what He provides.

It's all right here — daily bread, the promise of the future, the forgiveness of sins, peace and joy, the community and fellowship of the church, the Holy Spirit — to enable us to enjoy Him, to enjoy life, to enjoy ourselves. Let's eat, drink, and be merry, not because we die tomorrow but because we have an eternal life to enjoy!

Eucharistic People

The Scriptures are surprisingly relevant for people like us living in the 20th century and wanting to find enjoyment and excitement in life. Sometimes it is the least likely passage that proves to be the most promising. For example, the apostle Paul writes:

> Now the Spirit expressly says that in later times some will . . . forbid marriage and enjoin abstinence from foods which God created to be received with thanksgiving by those who believe and know the truth. For everything created by God is good, and nothing is to be rejected if it is received with thanksgiving; for then it is consecrated by the Word of God and prayer. (1 Timothy 4:1-5)

There is something a bit strange about these words. The apostle tells us about people who forbid others from being married and who compel them to abstain from certain foods. We live in a world — certainly in a country — where taking wives and consuming food are no longer unique experiences; they have become just ordinary and commonplace occurrences of life.

While we may not live in a culture such as St. Paul shared, where some people believe that the pleasures of life must be rejected (a notion, by the way, which many Christian people still insist upon even in modern times), the problem today by far is that we have everything, as Luther put it: " . . . food, drink, clothing, shoes, house, home, field, cattle, money, goods," or as the man of the street might say, "Wine, women, and song," or as we are likely to see in print almost anywhere, "Sex and success." We are getting more but are enjoying it less. For multitudes today life doesn't seem to have a kick anymore.

What's the problem? There is no genuine celebration, no real thanksgiving. When we cannot receive anything as a gift from God, there are only two things we can do: we must despise it through non-use or dissipate it through over-use. These are two sides of the same problem. Many of the ancient pagans believed that material and physical things were not good, that they were created by an evil god. Apparently in St. Paul's days there was a movement under way — he calls it a "deceitful spirit" and a "doctrine of demons" — to minimize things involving the use of the body, and he cites sex and food. He points out that what these people are rejecting are the good things God has created.

The influence of asceticism has never been completely eliminated from the thinking and living of many Christians. We all know enough about the medieval days from our study of history to recall how terribly ascetic Christian people can be. The good life was the monastic life, where abstinence from sex and from eating and drinking was regarded as the God-pleasing thing. Today we retain enough of a Victorian spirit to make us feel guilty about the enjoyment of the body, preventing us from a thankful enjoyment of God's good gifts.

Contrary to popular opinion, the life the Bible recommends is not one of denying certain pleasures or despising basic human satisfactions but rather one of enjoying our earthly life. Very few people in the Bible were abstainers. John the Baptist was the ascetic of his day, the antisocial type. But Jesus Christ was different. And people saw the difference. They said that He "ate and drank." He was always eating with somebody, breaking bread and giving thanks, blessing the common use of ordinary things. He was a eucharistic person.

The richest heritage that He has left us is that of a meal, a fellowship together which actualizes communion with God and with one another. The Lord's Supper is an affirmation of life, a celebration of that life we have with God through the forgiving presence of Christ. It involves enjoyment of the body as much as of the spirit.

Despite the fact that St. Paul was a man of unusual self-control, he was to a considerable degree a man of the world. He was another one of those eucharistic people who enjoyed life. It is true, of course, that both Paul and Christ never married (they had personal reasons for that). Yet we can infer that for both Christ and Paul a wedding banquet and the sexual union of man and woman were symbols of the excitement and enjoyment of life with God.

It follows, then, that if we cannot find joy by rejecting life, we cannot find enjoyment by seizing it either. That seems to be the modern approach. We want to get the most out of living these days. We eat and drink and play; we buy and build; we use. But we also plunder and waste, we spend and dissipate. We have fun, but we do not always have enjoyment. We idolize marriage, career, business success, social status, trying to find in these things something that will give us a kick. But it never happens that way. Instead of finding joy in God — which is what thanksgiving is — people try to find joy in something less than God. When life is recognized as received from God, it brings enjoyment, because the joy is in God and not simply in what God gives.

There is something else to consider. We cannot overlook the fact that the people who seem to enjoy life less are not necessarily those who have little to eat and drink, or those who have never married. There may be greater suffering today among those who are married and those who do eat and drink. It is difficult for the person with a marital problem, a drinking problem, and an eating problem to give thanks, to enjoy life. The very things which are supposed to be something good in his life have become evil. How can that kind of life be received with thanksgiving?

The way out of our trouble is not by despising what God has made, the things and the people He has given to us, nor by giving in to the evil that surrounds us. The way out comes through His grace in Jesus Christ, by the promise of life and forgiveness and reconciliation through Him, so that in the midst of our evil we might still find joy in God and give thanks to Him.

How urgent it is for us to recover a note of joy in our living! In a world of plenty, in an age of progress, at a time of prosperity we are a people fast becoming choked by all that we enjoy. Having it all taken from us is not necessarily the answer. Only one thing can keep us from destroying ourselves and turning the good things of God into a curse and can change us into eucharistic people: the goodness of God.

In his Letter to the Romans (2:4b) the apostle Paul raises the question, "Do you not know that God's kindness is meant to lead you to repentance?" We cannot give thanks for life, we cannot enjoy our living unless we know the goodness of God in it. And such a life is possible for us because of Jesus Christ.

When we begin to think that being born and living in the world as human beings is some kind of curse, then we should behold in the coming of Christ God's blessing upon human life. In Jesus we see that life is good, that God likes it. And that means that we can begin to enjoy it also.

When we begin to think that everything seems to be going to pot and crumbling under our feet, that our existence is shot through with sin and corruption; when we catch ourselves saying, "What's the use!" God comes to us with all His goodness in Word and promise, assuring us that He loves us. He showed us in the healing ministry of Christ that He has the power to make people new and whole again. He revealed to us in decisive fashion His ability to redeem the world and renew the whole earth by raising Jesus Christ from the dead. In these acts God has put joy into our living, enabling us to receive all things from Him in thanksgiving.

Eucharistic people — that's what He turns us into. The word "eucharistic" is a transliteration of a Greek term which appears rather frequently in the New Testament. It means "to rejoice," "to give thanks." It is a term that is associated with a celebration, a feast, a festival. It is, curiously enough, the name which the early church gave to the Lord's Supper — the Eucharist, the thanksgiving, the celebration!

What has happened to this dimension? It is a fact that we have obscured it with a false sense of piety. We have turned religion into a sacrifice instead of a service. We have made worship a duty rather than a party. It's time, then, to get caught up in a new spirit. We are eucharistic people, touched by the goodness of God in Christ, finding His blessing upon the whole of life, upon our entire earthly day-to-day existence. Christian worship and Christian Communion is a way of bringing these lives we live into the very presence of Christ and returning them to the world to enjoy what God has given.

In All Things Thanksgiving

What at last is the sign that God is alive, that He is present in our lives? What at last reveals that there is a Creator and Provider, that each of us has a heavenly Father? What shows us that this is not a big, empty world filled with things and machines and natural events, a few cheers and mostly sighs, that life is a pulsating, purposeful experience? Is it the sight of waving fields of grain? Is it a beautiful flower? Is it the moonshots? Is it the birth of a baby? Is it your new home or your new raise? Are these the signs that God is alive?

All these are indeed things which we recognize as God's gifts to us and for which we give thanks. But these things are not the sign of His presence, simply because these things cannot speak His praises, cannot express joy and thanksgiving.

The sign of God's presence in the world is people who celebrate and give thanks in all things. We are the sign that God is alive, that He provides, that He gives meaning to our lives. It is through people that God reveals Himself. It is through our joyful response to God that the world knows that He is.

A perceptive Christian told me once that what the world needs, what the church needs, is human beings who can really be human, who can live in this world with all their thoughts and feelings and experiences and really enjoy life. That is an accurate analysis. There are too many Christian people who are inhibited and afraid, unable to let go, unwilling to plunge themselves joyfully into the adventure of life, unprepared to embrace the whole of life — the good and the bad, the pleasure and the pain, the beauty and the tragedy of it — with joy and thanksgiving.

Sometimes the very place and setting in which one would expect to find an expression of joy and thanksgiving — in a service of praise — is devoid of the sign of God's presence. Let's face it, there is something stiff and unnatural about the way we enter church and participate in the service. There is an artificial, forced kind of solemnity or piety about our church behavior, as though natural feelings, the human element, had no place in what we do. Where are the spontaneity, the smiles, the laughter, the physical contact? Is the experience of God something sad and solemn? The Sacrament, the Breaking of Bread, the act of fellowship and sharing, has become a sterile thing, and for some people — you can see it on their faces — a sign of pain. In all things thanksgiving?

The things Christians do together in their worship are intended to be a kind of stimulation for joyful, thankful living. However, it often seems to have the opposite effect. It is no secret that many who call themselves Christians receive more stimulation for living the joyous life from such movies like *Tom Jones* and *Zorba the Greek,* from the music of the Beatles or the Tijuana Brass, from the excitement of a football game, from the fellowship of the bowling alley or the local pub than from all the theology and liturgy, the hymns and preaching of the church put together. Are we approaching the time when secular forms will shape our joy and praise rather than the worship action of the church?

Should that day ever come — and some people believe it has already arrived — who then will be a joyful witness to the presence of God? Who will celebrate as a means of praising God and building up other people in their faith in God? He who cannot give thanks in this thing — in the Word of God, in the person of Jesus Christ — finally cannot give thanks at all. We can achieve a certain kind of happiness without the

Word of God, a happiness that at last consumes itself, but we cannot be happy in God without His Word, without His Christ, the greatest human sign of His presence.

Thanksgiving in all things must begin in the first thing, in the Word that comes into our midst as we gather together. So St. Paul writes: "Let the Word of Christ dwell in you richly, as you teach and admonish one another in all wisdom, and as you sing psalms and hymns and spiritual songs with thankfulness in your hearts to God." (Colossians 3:16)

As Martin Luther confessed, Jesus Christ, "true God, begotten of the Father from eternity, and also true man, born of the Virgin Mary, is my Lord." He is the one who makes God real to us because He carries the love of the Father into our world. But He also makes us real, makes us true human beings, because He was a man.

I will never forget the day a woman told me that even though I was a pastor I was still human because I had skin and hair as anyone else. Well, Jesus was fully human, and God's sending Him to us as a real man is His blessing of our humanity. Furthermore, the Lord dies as a man and rises again as a new man because God loves man. This is our joy: We are one with God through Jesus Christ. In Christ God knows the exhaustion of human life; in Christ we know the everlastingness of life with God.

48260

This Christ, who is the Word of God, is the One who lives among us, who loves us, who meets us in sermon and sacrament and song. He is the One whom we love, whom we share in the Supper. God gives us Christ and we respond in thanksgiving, in acts of praise, in the joy of being together, touching one another, talking to one another. We have the sign of the presence of God in the world in Jesus Christ, our Lord and our Brother. Thanksgiving in all things starts with this thing, with this Word.

But it doesn't end there. Thanksgiving in that thing is thanksgiving in all things, in every circumstance and situation in life. St. Paul continues: "And whatever you do, in word or deed, do everything in the name of the Lord Jesus, giving thanks to God the Father through Him" (Colossians 3:17). We need to be able to receive life, to respect it and enjoy it. That's what it means to be a man, to be truly human — to love God and to love people.

In Jesus Christ God has shown the world what life is all about. He has made plain once and for all that man has been created to be in His image here on earth, the image of justice and mercy and love, a co-worker in God's history, and a caretaker of God's good earth. To be a child of God is to be a human being who enjoys and preserves all the good things of life, who rejoices with all men in the possession of life.

25

When we become such new creatures of God, we ourselves, in the likeness of our Lord, become signs of His presence in the world.

When we truly do our thing as we worship with God's people, when we share the Lord thankfully with one another in a very human way, in a very natural, simple way, then we are prepared to do our thing everywhere. We are then able to engage in "thanksliving" with a sense of joy, with a feeling of unity and harmony with all things and all people because of Jesus Christ.

Why shouldn't we? As John Elliott has described so strikingly in his book *The Christ Life:*

> And why shouldn't God's beautifying of the world through Jesus Christ be celebrated not only through the grace and beauty of the sacraments but also in our daily living to which these sacraments give power and style? Why shouldn't we Christians develop a "lipstick and rouge, soap and shaving lotion" theology? To adorn the new creation, to doll up the new man and the new woman, to swing to the tunes that make us happy and bring back pleasant memories, to enjoy an artist's vision, to delight in the beauty of a woman or the handsomeness of a man, to open our

eyes and ears and senses to all the marvels of God's lovely creation—how can this be "unfitting" to the people who claim to have known God's grace and glory in the Man of the world, Jesus of Nazareth? (Pp. 65—66)

Well, then, let us give thanks as we sing hymns and spiritual songs, as we share bread and wine, as we offer ourselves, because Christ is present wherever people gather in His name. But let us also give thanks in whatever we do in work and play, in our tears, in our celebrations, in our failures and successes, in everything. We are signs of the presence of God. Therefore in all things thanksgiving!

Eating and Drinking as Celebration

Martin Luther said somewhere that God is rich in His grace toward the children of men. He was emphasizing not so much the fact that God has lots of love for people, but rather that He has a variety of ways in which He communicates His love to us. The eating and drinking of the Lord's Supper is one of those means.

With remarkable simplicity Luther defined the Sacrament of the Altar as

> ". . . the true body and blood of our Lord Jesus Christ"—not a facsimile, a Jesus in the spirit, a representation, a figure of speech, but the Lord really, fully, truly, completely, totally present;
> ". . . under the bread and wine"—through ordinary elements that we can chew and swallow, through substances that remain what they are and have always been, by means of physical, material, earthly things;
> ". . . for us Christians"—for no one else

but those who believe in Him and follow Him, who call Him Lord and Savior; not just for anybody who believes there is a God and who may have a desire to follow the good life, but for those who know God and His goodness in the mighty death and resurrection of God's Son;

". . . to eat and drink"—to take Christ in not only by reading the Word or hearing the Word but by receiving Him orally;

". . . instituted by Christ Himself"—not a legacy of the apostles, not a tradition of the church, not an arrangement of men, but a means of grace and life from the hand of our Lord Himself.

As such this meal is more than a "private little absolution." It is an experience that stands at the center of Christian worship and life, rich in meaning and power for our lives. In this chapter and in the three succeeding ones we want to explore the depth of this blessed Sacrament as implied in the words of Luther referred to above and as expressly taught in the New Testament. We shall view the eating and drinking as celebration, participation, anticipation, and thanksgiving. Our concern in this chapter is with the eating and drinking as celebration.

There should not be much question that the note of celebration needs to be recovered today, not only in our approach to worship but also in our approach to life. Much in the world discourages and depresses us: family discord, racial unrest, international tensions. Unfortunately religion seems to have increased fear and guilt in people rather than helping them to deal with these problems constructively, rather than injecting into our lives a sense of joy. As Richard Luecke has stated in his book *New Meanings for New Beings:*

> Unless one celebrates now, in whatever circumstances, he may never really celebrate at all. Unless one celebrates something besides his own feelings, he may have nothing to celebrate at all. We may be all for self-expression but have we nothing to express besides ourselves? At a time when men are either numbly silent or else feverishly busy expressing themselves in the face of personal and universal death, someone had better remember to celebrate! (P. 252)

St. Paul wrote to the Christians in the city of Corinth, "Let us, therefore, celebrate the festival" (1 Corinthians 5:8a). He was speaking, of course, in terms of the Passover, but was alluding also to the Holy Communion which superseded the Passover celebration. Whether we take his words to refer to the Passover (which for Christians had become Easter) or to the Eucharist, we understand them as an invitation to celebrate Christ.

What Christ did was celebration. His very presence in the world was an occasion for festive joy, from the *Gloria in Excelsis* of the angels at the time of His birth to the words of the Father at the time of His baptism and transfiguration: "This is My beloved Son in whom I am well pleased."

When Jesus healed the sick and raised the dead, announcing that the kingdom of God had come, He was celebrating the power of God over the forces of sickness and death. In His parables, like the stories of the lost sheep, the lost coin and the lost son, He taught that there is joy in heaven among the angels when a sinner repents, that God is happy when His forgiving love transforms a suffering soul. Furthermore our Lord was one who ate and drank with sinners, with the rejects of society. He celebrated with people the healing presence of God, imparting that presence Himself, for He was the One through whom the Father was pleased to redeem the world.

One night, during the celebration of the Passover, Jesus gathered His disciples and instituted a new form of eating and drinking.

Even though that was a night to say farewells, there was celebration in the air. The people of Israel had a good memory. They recalled without fail the great redemptive act of God in their history — how He delivered them from slavery in Egypt, how He gave them an identity and the promise of the future. In this victory celebration they relived the Exodus, reciting the covenant God had made with them.

Remembering was God's unique nature. Whenever He remembered, promises were fulfilled. Jesus knew that well. He knew what He was doing that night when He inaugurated a new chapter in God's history with men. During the course of the meal He arose, took the blessed bread and wine, and distributed the food and drink to His disciples with the words: "Take, eat, this is My body"; "take, drink, this cup is the New Testament in My blood, shed for you for the remission of sins." He celebrates the grace of God in the face of those horrible hours that were upon Him. The thought of the cross did not deter Him. If God's life must be celebrated in the world by means of His death, it shall be so. If it is God's deed, then it must bring victory.

When St. Paul urges us to "celebrate the festival," he is inviting us to pick up life from that point. The new age has begun; "Christ, our Paschal Lamb, has been sacrificed!" Christ doesn't die anymore; the victory is His. The power of sin and Satan and death has been beaten down forever. As the Israelites fled Egypt, spared from the avenging angel of death because of the blood of sacrificial lambs that marked their doorposts, so the Christ who offered His body and shed His blood for all people accomplished a new deliverance. In an Easter hymn Martin Luther put it this way:

> Here the true Paschal Lamb we see,
> Whom God so freely gave us;
> He died on the accursed tree —
> So strong His love! — to save us.
> See, His blood doth mark our door;
> Faith points to it, death passes o'er,
> And Satan cannot harm us. Hallelujah!

The Christian life is essentially a celebration. We cannot stress this too much. There are too many interpretations of Christianity that are negative, confining, narrow, where sorrow over sin, fear of punishment, obedience to the Law, and insistence on duty have become the guiding principles. We are not suggesting, of course, that now we can gloss over sin and the commandments and the sting of death. We are simply asserting that we are no longer captive to these powers, even though we commit sin and break commandments and suffer death. Our Lord lives with the power to save, and therefore our living from here on is a celebration of forgiveness in the midst of sin, of justification before the accusations of the Law, of eternal life in the face of death. No matter how weak we may become, no matter how hopeless things may seem, life is still a festival, a victory celebration. God, who always has the last word, has seen to that!

What is Christian worship but a reciting with praise what God has done and is still doing for us in Jesus Christ? What else could it be basically but a remembering with joy the power and presence of the living Christ who feeds and strengthens us for the living of His life in the world? Christians gather as a family around Word and Sacrament because they believe that life is worth celebrating.

That Christian worship is not always a celebration is easy to demonstrate. The eating and drinking have become a commemoration of the confession of sins, a solemnizing of sorrow instead of a celebration of the forgiveness of sins. It has become this even though we continue to use the verb "celebrate" to describe the action that takes place in the Lord's Supper. Everything in the Communion liturgy, which we enact again and again, points to a celebration: "Lift up your hearts!" "Holy, holy, holy!" "Do this in remembrance of Me!" "The peace of the Lord be with you alway!" And still we have long faces, bowed heads, drooping spirits. Anything but a celebration!

We will suggest a reason why this happens. Have we come to believe that it is not quite Christian to enjoy life, to rejoice before the altar, because the world is too sinful and we are too sinful, and the only thing that really pleases God is to repent and feel sorry and grovel before Him? If so, this means that the Christian life is a negative affair, a sad, somber experience. It means that the more solemn our worship and the more sorrowful our eating and drinking, the more Christian it is. And that is a monstrous heresy! It is a refusal to rejoice in the things of God, to celebrate in the world what Christ spreads before His people.

When we come together to eat and drink, we come to make merry. We look up and ahead. The past is behind; the future is before us. Confession is behind, and sorrow with it. We live in the presence of Christ, where there is forgiveness, life, and salvation. The time then is not for commiserating but for celebrating!

There is, of course, a proper place for confession and contrition. I would submit that there can be no true celebration without genuine confession. But why mingle confession and celebration at the Lord's Table? In the days of the early church, and even up to the time of Martin Luther, confession of sins and absolution were experienced privately before the pastor. And that was almost a sacrament in itself, a part of the ongoing life of the Christian under the grace of God. However, when the Protestant church, contrary to Luther's intention, replaced private confession with general confession such as most churches have now (in many ways still a healthy experience), the unfortunate consequence was that confession and not celebration set the tone for worship and Holy Communion. What is worse, it later became part of the preparation—even a requirement—as one readied himself for participation in the Lord's Supper. The result today is that people are hung up with fear and guilt, with whether they are sorry enough, whether they might misuse the Sacrament, whether they feel right about God or about themselves. And when we approach the Table by starting with ourselves, with our feelings, with our own piety or lack of it, with our habits and traditions instead of with God and His Christ, then what we do will be something less than celebration.

Above anything else eating and drinking with Christ and with other Christians is a free, festive occasion. Having the Word that God loves us and that Christ is with us, living with the Good News that the Lord, once sacrificed for sin, is now alive to bless us, we are able to celebrate. The world has been redeemed and reclaimed for God, and we are His people invited to eat and drink in His kingdom, to find joy in Him. How then can we keep from making every service of worship on the Lord's Day an eating and drinking in celebration? How can we hold back from jumping into the action whenever the Sacrament is being celebrated? How can we walk out or simply sit and pass it by without thereby refusing to celebrate the festival of Christ? Here is the opportunity to relive our history, to revive our daily calling as well as recall our hope for heaven.

From that hymn again:

> So let us keep the festival
> Whereto the Lord invites us;
> Christ is Himself the Joy of all,
> The Sun that warms and lights us.
> By His grace He doth impart
> Eternal sunshine to the heart;
> The night of sin is ended. Hallelujah!

Eating and Drinking as Participation

Martin Luther was an individualist if there ever was one, a man of courageous character who could stand alone against Satan and even against the church. So firm was his faith, so strong his self-identity! It was he who said that every man must do his own believing, his own dying; who said that when a man hears the Word of God and when he celebrates the Lord's Supper, he must believe that Christ is for him as though there were no one else around.

Because of Luther's high regard for the individual he has become a model for modern man. Even today in our society rugged individualism is still considered the supreme good. Most of us feel that when the importance of the individual is lost, democracy and even civilization goes down the drain.

We likewise believe that Protestantism and certainly Lutheranism will disappear unless we retain the theology that every man has his own dignity and freedom before God, that every man may approach Christ by means of his faith without the priestly system of the church. The great Protestant value is the importance of the individual.

It is unfortunate, however, that we do not always see this in focus. Luther would be horrified to discover what we have done to his doctrine of the individual. While he held high the importance of the individual and the freedom of the Christian man, he never thought of a person apart from community, whether marriage, family, society, or the church. For him a person was something less than a true individual if he could not function within the human relationships God had provided for him. So, any idea of people existing alone as though fellowship were unnecessary was a denial of the freedom and the life which Christ won for us.

An individualism that becomes nonparticipation is a selfish and an empty approach to life. When the great value becomes self-importance or self-sufficiency, we destroy the individual — ourselves and others — because true individuality is impossible apart from community. The emotionally undernourished child cannot emerge from his family experiences as a strong individual. He must spend his life searching for security. And when he marries he does not participate in a relationship; he exploits instead. Black men — or members of some other minority group — cannot emerge as a responsible people from a society that does not accept them. If they lack a sense of community, they lack a sense of individuality and identity. The chances are they will end up destroying rather than contributing. Participation is the path to individual strength.

Those who are most capable of fulfilling the demands of marriage and community life are those who have the strongest feelings of being accepted, who have learned to share their deepest anxieties, who have learned to relate, who have learned to love.

The fact of the matter is that Luther was a great individual because he was close to mother church. Whatever complaints he had against the papacy about the excesses of the institutional church, he knew that no one had an identity with Christ, an individual relationship with his Lord, apart from the church. Essential to our lives as persons before God is the opportunity for Christian community, for the fellowship where Christians give strength to one another.

The church exists to provide that fellowship with Christ and one another which we all need along the way of life to grow as persons, as members of the body of Christ. Within the community of the church the eating and drinking of the Lord's Supper is the basic form of participation.

In his First Letter to the Corinthian congregation St. Paul writes: "Because there is one loaf, we who are many are one body, for we all partake of the same loaf" (1 Corinthians 10:17). Here he refers to the action by which the many become one, by which the church grows and functions as the body of Christ. Later in the same letter (12:27) he says: "Now you are the body of Christ and individually members of it." In his Letter to the Romans he leaves no doubt about what he means: "For as in one body we have many members, and all the members do not have the same function, so we, though many, are one body in Christ, and individually members of one another" (Romans 12:4, 5). His diagram is plain: the body is nothing without the individual members; the individual member is nothing without the body. As Paul describes it, the remarkable unity and harmony that exist within the parts of the human body illustrate the fellowship of the church, where Christians participate in Christ and in one another. There's no choosing between being an individual or becoming a part of the group; there's no danger of losing one's individuality within the community. It's always a matter of reaching maturity as an individual member within the family of the church and the body of Christ.

Notice that St. Paul does not talk about Christian fellowship in the abstract, for he connects it to the eating and drinking of the Communion Meal. He insists that to eat the bread is to participate in the body of Christ; to drink the cup is to participate in the blood of Christ (1 Corinthians 10:16). Because Lutherans have always believed that the bread and the wine in the Sacrament are really the body and blood of Christ rather than some symbolic representation, we tend to interpret these words of St. Paul to mean exclusively that when the individual member communes at the Lord's Table he receives the true body and blood of the Lord. But the apostle is arguing for something else as well. The difficulty in the Corinthian church was not its lack of understanding about the Real Presence but its lack of perception regarding the consequences of the eating and drinking. The Corinthians ignored the fact that at the Lord's Table Christians become what they eat. As a member of the body of Christ the Christian becomes one with all other members; he participates in the fellowship and communion of saints.

A meal has always been a concrete expression of fellowship. When is a family most a family? When it is sharing a meal together, of course. Why are restaurants the world over still an attraction for tourists and native alike? Because the atmosphere of food and drink is conducive to fellowship, of course. Man cannot exist without fellowship.

Those who criticized Jesus knew what eating and drinking together meant. They protested His eating and drinking with sinners because that was having fellowship with people whom they thought He should avoid. To them this was a scandal. To those, however, who shared the company of the Lord this was grace and forgiveness.

So it is in the eating and drinking of the Lord's Supper. Something happens to people when they are permitted to share in His Meal. They experience a oneness, a healing. Because we have in the Sacrament the gift of the Lord's presence, we discover what the unity of the church is. We are able to recognize one another as brothers; we grow in love and concern for one another. When we feed together on the Bread of Life Himself we are restored to the community, to the healing of the body of Christ.

In describing this action St. Paul uses the metaphor of the loaf and the cup. Luther elaborates on this:

> Now it is true that we Christians are the Spiritual Body of Christ and are together one Bread, one Cup, one Spirit. Christ accomplishes this, who through His own Body makes us all one Spiritual Body, so that we all become partakers of His Body alike and thus also are members one of another. . . . For out of many

grains of wheat which are ground together comes one bread and each grain loses its own form and becomes flour to the other; likewise many berries become one wine and each berry loses its own form and becomes wine to the other. So Christ has become all to us and we, each one, have become all to the others when we are Christians.

Can it be denied that this dimension of eating and drinking needs to be recovered in the life of the church? It seems that for many people the church is not a family but a place to which the individual returns from time to time for private meditation or for an occasional ritual. Even the Lord's Supper has become a private communion within a public setting. So steeped are some people in this approach, and so individualistic is their attitude, that their life in the church and their attendance at the Lord's Table are anything but participation. This attitude often turns out to be something like that of the child who refuses to come to the supper table, or of the man who refuses relations with his wife, or of the citizen who is concerned only with his own rights. It's like the attitude of people who don't need people.

And people who come to the Lord's Table like that do not fully share in the Lord's body. They commune with blinders on, seeing only themselves and their own needs, controlled by their own feelings or habits, unmindful of the needs of their brother and the total community. This is the situation to which the apostle refers when he takes the Corinthian Christians to task:

> It follows, then, that if anyone eats the Lord's bread or drinks from his cup in an improper manner, he is guilty of sin against the Lord's body and blood. . . . For if he does not recognize the meaning of the Lord's body when he eats the bread and drinks from the cup, he brings judgment on himself as he eats and drinks.
>
> (1 Corinthians 11:27, 29)

This is true when one pretends to participate. How much more it would be true when one refuses to participate. For then, whatever his reasons, he despises the Food and Drink as well as his fellows, both his Lord and his brothers, in whom and with whom he shares the forgiveness of sins.

Our Lord is present with His church through the Meal to reach the individual, to give each of us an identity as a member of His body, to make each of us His very flesh and blood. It was for each of us that He died and now lives to save, to heal us, to restore us by means of the fellowship He communicates through the Meal. The Lord comes to us not in isolation or in a vacuum but through the community. He shares all things with us, takes all of our sins and weaknesses upon Himself, only to impart to us the common gift of His life and health. Eating and drinking are participation, Christ participating in our lives and we participating in His.

Everyone, the strong one and the weak one alike, needs meaningful, supportive experiences. We find them in the community of the Sacrament. Identification with Christ and His church brings release from fear and judgment, restores us to a healthy regard for self, fills us with love for God and our neighbor. The eating and drinking lifts us out of our isolation and loneliness and gives us a sense of belonging. In this Meal we participate in what we have become, what God has made us to be—the many becoming one, the lost finding a home, the sufferer finding rest, the individual discovering himself in the living Christ, the community of the church moving toward fulfillment as the body of Christ.

Eating and Drinking as Anticipation

Describing modern man Viktor Frankl has said that we are not dominated by the will-to-pleasure, nor by the will-to-power, but by a longing and a striving to find a will-to-meaning.

Even Friedrich Nietzsche, the nihilist, said, "If a man has a why for his life he can bear with almost any how."

Albert Camus speaks through a character in one of his books: "Here is what frightens me, to lose one's life is a little thing, and I will have the courage when necessary. But to see the sense of this life dissipated, to see our reason for existence disappear, that is what is intolerable. And man cannot live without meaning."

One day a woman, her marriage a wreck and her children showing evidence of a warped view of life, told me, "I've got to start all over somewhere; I've got to find out who I am and why I am here."

Perhaps in one way or another each of us can identify with this anxiety of meaninglessness. Whatever our personal experience in life, one thing is sure: We have a common longing of fulfillment. We live every day aware of physical and social disintegration. We see what happens to the body through disease and death. We behold the forces that dismember the corporate body of man socially and racially. We observe how the body of Christ, the church, suffers from its divisions and separations.

It is then that we look toward the day when all this will be no more, when man and his community and his universe will be healed. When we have something to look forward to, some hope of personal and universal fulfillment, we can live, we can face our problems, we can do our work, we can raise our families. When there is a quality of anticipation about our lives, we are able to keep going, to struggle on with a sense of meaning and hope.

Eating and drinking in the Lord's Supper provides us with that sense. St. Paul teaches us, "For as often as you eat this bread and drink the cup, you proclaim the Lord's death until he comes" (1 Corinthians 11:26). The Meal as anticipation is the living Christ leading His church to ultimate healing in the resurrection. We who eat and drink together find in that moment of our lives a future. As we look back upon the event of the cross, as we look ahead to our Lord's return in glory, we have hope.

Not everyone lives with a sense of anticipation. We know, for example, how it is possible for people to live only in the past. The disillusioned tend to live by memories, if they have any. For such the present is a burden and the future is an uncertainty. The only things that seem to give their lives any meaning are the experiences of the past. And life in the past tense has no anticipation.

On the other hand, there are those who say that they live for the moment. They are caught up in present concerns. The past does not seem to bother them, including their mistakes and failures. Convinced that they cannot do anything about it anyhow, they want rather to make the most of the present. Not at all sure that there will be a future, a tomorrow, they don't want to miss out on the opportunities for living right now. They live in the present tense. But a life that has no continuity, no history linking people with the past or pointing them toward the future, sooner or later becomes an in-between existence subject to emptiness and meaninglessness. The quality of anticipation is missing.

Another kind of people may be classified as future-oriented, people who live with a certain kind of expectancy. They are hoping (or should we say dreaming?) that their luck will change. Multitudes today look for the next day, the next job, the next break. Youth and middle-aged eagerly await something big just around the corner which when it happens will change everything. The trouble with that kind of expectancy is that it has no basis in fact. It is nothing more than wishful thinking. It is not really anticipation; it is anxiety.

The tragedy of a life that gets buried in the past or present or future is not that we get our tenses mixed up, that we are immature or disoriented, but that we are unable to live with any sense of God. Though God is not one who is controlled or limited by the tenses of time, nevertheless He is the One who gives meaning to our past, our present, our future. He makes possible a sense of anticipation about life because He became involved in our times. Not only has He created all things, He has also redeemed everything and has promised to restore all things.

This action centers in Jesus Christ. It is in Him that our lives take on meaning. It is because of His involvement in our life situation that we have a history, a continuity, a destiny. It is by Him that our lives move toward fulfillment.

The eating and drinking of the Lord's Supper supplies the framework in which our anticipation finds substance. The Meal which our Lord has left us is three-dimensional. It is, first of all, a celebration in the present. St. Paul's words "For as often as you eat this bread and drink the cup" refer to the present moment. Right now we have the living Christ. He is not before us or beyond us; He is with us.

But the One who lives with us and for us is the Lord who died. Out of the past comes the power of His death. That is why Paul wrote, "You proclaim the Lord's death" whenever you eat and drink. It is not so much that in the Supper we are remembering what our Savior did for us, for then we would be turning the Sacrament into a memorial meal. And it certainly cannot mean that in this Sacrament the Lord is sacrificed again. There could be no eucharistic celebration without a powerful victory over death, without a sacrifice complete, once and for all—and for always! In the eating and drinking we experience His mighty death and resurrection as He brings His risen life to bear upon ours.

And all of this "until He comes." Our Lord invites us to participate with Him in the Meal that proclaims His present power and His future glory. Those who eat with Him and upon Him are on their way towards fulfillment. As we eat and drink we look to the end of all things with joy in our hearts.

Ignatius of Antioch (early 2nd century bishop and martyr) called the Lord's Supper a "medicine of immortality." Martin Luther, repeating this idea, reminds that the believer is made alive by the body and blood of the Lord. We recall his explanation of the benefits of eating and drinking:

> That is shown us by these words, "Given, and shed for you for the remission of sins"; namely, that in the Sacrament forgiveness of sins, life, and salvation are given us through these words. For where there is forgiveness of sins, there is also life and salvation.

Or consider this in his explanation to the Third Article:

> . . . in which Christian church He daily and richly forgives all sins to me and all believers, and will at the last day raise up me and all the dead, and give unto me and all believers in Christ eternal life. . . .

Instructive, furthermore, are these statements from his commentary on Jesus' words in John 6: "I am the Living Bread which came down from heaven; if any one eats of this bread, he will live forever":

> [The flesh of Christ] is an imperishable, immortal, indestructible flesh. . . . Once death tried to consume and devour it, but it could not. The flesh of Christ tore

the stomach and threat of death into more than a hundred thousand pieces, so that death's teeth were pulled out and thrown away; but it [the flesh of Christ] remained alive. For the food was too strong for death, and the food consumed and devoured the eater. God is present in this flesh, it is a spirit-flesh. It is in God and God is in it; therefore, it is alive itself, and it gives life to all who eat it, both to the body and the soul.

Thus the great Reformer is teaching that in our eating and drinking the resurrected life of our Lord takes shape among His people. As we share in the Meal, the Lord both nourishes us with His body and blood as life for the present and prepares us for life in the resurrection. The forgiveness of sins which our Lord accomplished by means of the cross is not just something that brings peace at the moment when we are troubled by our sins and guilt, but it is also the promise and assurance of eternal life. To participate in the Lord's Supper is to anticipate our own resurrection, for in the eating and drinking the Lord keeps His people intact, signaling the day of His return and the consummation of all things.

"Where there is forgiveness of sins, there is also life and salvation," wrote Martin Luther

in his Small Catechism. There is a vast spacious-
ness and roominess in God's love. That is salvation. It does not refer to some kind of individual
survival but to the healing of the whole man, the
whole church, the whole order of things. This
gift and promise we have in Jesus' resurrection,
a life and power at work in our own lives now,
especially as we eat and drink. The course we
travel by faith leads us in the direction of God's
future, for when He who is our Head returns to
raise His members, we will know the fullness of
salvation. If such is the goal of human existence,
then surely our living now has meaning and
purpose.

Precisely because we have anticipation,
because we know what God wills for us ulti-
mately, because we experience the healing of
Christ already in the sacramental eating and
drinking, we are able to work for the healing
of the body. The resurrection of Christ keeps
us at bringing relief to the suffering, seeking
solutions to poverty, discovering cures to disease; keeps us at working toward the recovery
of community and the elimination of racism;
keeps us at working toward unity until the time
when all sectarianism and separatism will no
longer disrupt life in the body of Christ.

The future has been given to us already,
and not to work toward some realization of it
is to deny it. For to anticipate what God will

yet give us means to participate in what He is doing now. We are not yet what we are meant to be, but we are on the way. What we shall be we have in Jesus Christ, and we eat and drink with Him and one another because we anticipate receiving at the heavenly banquet the promise of Him who wills to give us all things.

Thus our eating and drinking in the Communion Meal provides an antidote to one of the pressing problems of our time: the search for meaning. Eating and drinking as anticipation enables us to overcome the desperation and despair so characteristic of modern living. God is indeed rich in His grace toward the children of men!

Eating and Drinking
as Thanksgiving

One of the positive effects of the Lord's Supper for modern living is the upgrading of the material order, making holy the life that God has provided. When our Lord took bread into His hands, broke it, and gave thanks, He was blessing our material, earthly existence. That He would use the common, ordinary stuff of life to communicate His presence says something about the creation, about our worldly existence, about the common, ordinary things we handle.

In the eating and drinking we lose our fear of nature, and our fussing over it. We are free from having to avoid it or despise it or worship it. We are able to use it, to enjoy, to give thanks for it.

Perhaps we are not materialistic enough when we eat and drink. Perhaps we are too religious, too pious, too subjective about the whole thing. Perhaps we are too ritualistic, too churchly, too other-worldly about the common

Meal our Lord has instituted. Perhaps we have removed it from life, made it into something superstitious and unreal.

Perhaps we have missed its basic, earthy meaning. Eating and drinking as thanksgiving opens up life, fits us with a different perspective about our daily lives, allows us to take Christ out of the church and into the world, frees us to be what He has made us to be: His body in the world. Dietrich Bonhoeffer, writing from a Nazi prison camp, has given us insight into this action:

> [The Christian] must therefore plunge himself into the life of a godless world, without attempting to gloss over its ungodliness with a veneer of religion or trying to transfigure it. He must live a "worldly" life and so participate in the suffering of God in the life of the world. He *may* live a worldly life as one emancipated from all false religions and obligations. To be a Christian does not mean to be religious in a particular way, to cultivate some particular form of asceticism (as a sinner, a penitent, or a saint), but to be a man.

To some people Bonhoeffer's language may sound all too strange and confusing. The meaning of his words, however, is not new to the New Testament nor to the practice of the early church. As a matter of fact, it isn't new to us either. It is just that the obvious has been obscured. But it's all in our Communion liturgy.

Perhaps we have made too little of the offertory in the liturgy, treating it like a response to the sermon instead of an introduction of our response to the presence of Christ as we offer our money, the intercessions, the bread and the wine, our very bodies as vessels for service to Christ and to the world He has redeemed. Perhaps we have glossed over the thanksgiving portions of the liturgy leading up to the eating and drinking and following it, intent on enjoying the things of the spirit rather than the things of the body. Perhaps we have minimized the presence and the use of the elements, the consecrating of them and the eating and drinking of them. In short, perhaps we have disconnected the Sacrament from life.

The Christian life is never a running away; it is a coming forward. When we enter a church to worship we do that not to escape the world but to face it. We are bold enough to come before God with the stain of the world, the stress of competition, the anxieties of making a living, the problems of technology, the fear of destruction, and then to lay it all upon Him. We would certainly like to present God with a much better world and a much better life. So we bear in mind that what we offer to Him is not what is lost but what He has redeemed. Were it not for the redemption of His Son, we could not have such boldness.

As difficult as it is for us to come forward as we are and with what we have, the absurdity of it all is that we do it with thanksgiving. In the liturgy this action begins with the offertory. Having gathered our offerings together — symbols of the strain of our nerves and the sweat of our brows, of the world we traffic in every day — and having presented upon the table the bread and the wine, we move forward to offer our prayers to God and our intercessions for one another, to consecrate the elements for the Eucharistic Meal in a spirit of thanksgiving, chanting the words:

> Create in me a clean heart, O God,
>   and renew a right spirit within me.
> Cast me not away from Thy presence,
>   and take not Thy Holy Spirit from me.
> Restore unto me the joy of Thy salvation;
>   and uphold me with Thy free spirit.
>   (Psalm 51:10-12)

Symbolically we are putting everything on the table: our common world, our common life, our common needs as an expression of thanksgiving to God, who has permitted us to live another week in the world; who has preserved us in our faith though we have suffered and died a little more in our work and worry; who has made us aware of the needs of the world in general and of our brethren in particular by giving us hope and love. We are able to do this because the world and everything in it belongs to God. We know that it is good, since He made it and redeemed it.

And so we take bread and wine into our hands as Christ did, we consecrate it as He directed, and then we share it. We give thanks as He did for the world of creation, for the gifts of God, and we pray that He would turn these simple, ordinary things into vehicles of His grace and make them bearers of His redeeming, saving power.

Every Christian family participates in a similar "sacramental" eating and drinking daily. When at home we gather around the table to share our daily bread, we offer the prayer: "Come, Lord Jesus, be our Guest, and let these gifts to us be blessed." Every meal reminds us of the Lord's Supper. The disciples saw the Lord in the breaking of the bread. We too recognize Him as the unseen Guest wherever we gather to share God's gifts with one another. Table fellowship at home is a unique Christian experience.

There are some very good reasons why Christians, like the Hebrew people of old, offer blessing and thanksgiving at mealtime. There is, of course, a practical point to it. Mealtime represents perhaps the only time that the family is together for prayer and fellowship during the week. It is a good thing worth preserving, because we know that Christ is present with His people where they live and with whom they live. Even if such is a once-a-day experience, it is Christian celebration and participation.

There is still another reason, aside from the example of our Lord, why Christians give thanks when they break bread. Indeed we pray at other times and on other occasions; and we give thanks for gifts other than the food we consume. No doubt we give thanks at mealtime because we sense that what we are giving thanks for is something more than bread and milk, meat and potatoes, vegetables and desserts. We remember also in a table prayer that what we consume is the product of our labor, of modern technology. Represented in our food and drink are all the things that sustain our daily lives, our livelihood, our abilities, our opportunities.

Daily bread is more than simple bread. For bread is symbolic of the basic requirements of our bodily life. When Martin Luther wanted to find a reason for giving thanks to God, he remembered the Creator:

61

God has made me and all creatures. . . .
He has given me my body and soul, eyes,
ears, and all my members, my reason
and all my senses, and still preserves
them; also clothing and shoes, meat and
drink, house and home, wife and children, fields, cattle, and all my goods. . . .
He defends me against all danger, and
guards and protects me from all evil. . . .

Even though we don't live in the same
culture as the Reformer did, we get the point.

In his explanation to the Fourth Petition
of the Lord's Prayer Luther observed that
"daily bread" refers to "good government,
good weather, peace, health, discipline, honor,
good friends, faithful neighbors, and the like,"
making it quite clear that when the Lord took
bread in His hands to spread a table before His
people, and when we take bread in our homes,
blessing it and giving thanks for it, He and
we are holding up to God the totality of His
creation.

In the sacramental eating and drinking
itself we could make that presentation much
clearer. We could use bread that was real.
Wafers, foreign to our everyday experience,
pressed in some ecclesiastical supply house,
and brought into the church—nobody knows
how—hardly symbolize the offering of our common lives. Perhaps the families of congregations

could take turns supplying the bread and wine purchased at the local store (or even prepared at home), bringing them forward at the time the ushers present the offerings.

Whatever kind of bread we use in our eating and drinking, we know that we are creatures who need to be fed, who have needs and drives, who must depend not only on nature for our well-being but especially on God. And there is no shame in that. On the contrary, that is one of the glories of being men — that we can receive gifts, that we can trust God. For if we must make ourselves managers of the universe, or if we must either despise or worship the creation, then we are not in concert with God or with nature but are full of fear and anxiety and guilt. From this, however, we have been set free by a Lord, who did not despise either us or the things of life, who by His sacrifice presented us and all things to God as redeemed, as reclaimed from the power of the Evil One. His offering of Himself enables us to come forward in thanksgiving as we seek a blessing.

What we bring to God is His good creation now broken by sin and beset by death, but we return from the Table with the world intact, with the experience of healing. Our thanksgiving in the eating and drinking lies not only in our bringing ourselves and our world before God; it lies also in our receiving the blessings of a new life and expressing this new happening in "thanksliving."

Something happens to the world when Christ touches it. On the night in which He was betrayed our Lord took bread, gave thanks for it, and then consecrated it for a holy use. The bread, the grain of the earth and the stuff of life, would bear His true body to His church and, through the members of His church, into the life of the world. That He chose to use bread to feed us with Himself as the Bread of Life makes the bread something other than simple, ordinary bread. The same is true of the wine, through which He conveys His true blood.

What could be ordinary and simple about what God makes and redeems? In His Supper Christ discloses what creation is and what it is for. The material order is not a naked, mysterious power; not a vast, impersonal system; not a regime of relentless, monotonous laws. It is God's creation which He has made and in which He chooses to abide. It is the sphere where we do our living, our struggling, our dying; where His Son did His thing; where He demonstrated His power over the forces that held the Father's creation captive; where He brought His healing Word. That's how Christ gives thanks. That's how God blesses bread and wine.

And that's how we get offered up to God as living sacrifices. When we eat and drink we get caught up in the new creation. When we move out we not only carry the spiritual life of Christ in our hearts but also that consecrated and consumed bread and wine in our bodies to live consecrated lives. Thus St. Paul writes to the church at Rome:

> I appeal to you therefore, brethren, by the mercies of God, to present your bodies as a living sacrifice, holy and acceptable to God, which is your spiritual worship. Do not be conformed to this world but be transformed by the renewal of your mind, that you may prove what is the will of God, what is good and acceptable and perfect. (Romans 12:1-2)

Eating and drinking as thanksgiving produces a change in us so that we look at nature not as something to be abused but used to the glory of God; so that we view our daily calling and occupation not as something to be endured or belittled but to be undertaken as a challenge and an adventure; so that we see our bodies not to be dissipated or punished but hallowed and harnessed for service; so that we treat our fellow Christians not as things or tools but as children of God and members of the body of Christ. That is the kind of life we receive in the Sacrament—a compassionate, consecrated life of thanksgiving.

65

Eating and drinking as thanksgiving makes for a life of "thanksliving." The more we throw ourselves into the act of receiving and sharing Christ, the more of Him we will bear in our daily lives. We have received from the Lord a new way to live His grace and give thanks for His gifts. So whenever He gathers us together to break bread and to share His body, then nature and grace, the world and its Lord, become one. This is doing our eating and drinking, as Christ commands, "in remembrance of Me."

Soundness
of Health

In one of the collects we use occasionally for
the sick we pray "that they may be restored to
soundness of health, and give thanks to Thee in
Thy holy Church. . . ." The outcome of this petition has often occasioned great joy. There
are those whose songs of praise and thanksgiving
in the worship life of any congregation have been
interrupted by illness, and their recovery re-
sulted in a response of thanksgiving that brought
honor to God and joy to His people. There have
been others who had lost their desire or ability
to praise God, whose songs became silent, and
then a brush with death or a long illness awoke
them to God's saving power, and their lives become filled with thanksgiving in the church and
in the world.

For other people it hasn't always worked
out that way. On one occasion I ministered to
a man who awaited surgery — there was the possibility of cancer — and he was scared as anyone

of us would be. After it was all over and the biopsy proved negative, he told me, "You'll see me in church from now on." I am still waiting, and so is the church, because we interceded for him "that he may be restored to soundness of health and give thanks to Thee in Thy holy Church." Evidently thanksgiving doesn't always follow healing.

We recall Jesus' encounter with ten lepers. He healed all ten on the spot. Only one, we are told, came back to give praise to God. Surely all ten of them recognized that something had changed. When you are cured of a loathesome disease, when you can go home again and get back on the job, when you can enjoy living once more, you know that something has happened. But if it means nothing more than a change of circumstances, a person has missed something.

It doesn't take much for us to distort what happens in life. Pretty soon a man can see nothing but the "breaks" he gets in life. Pretty soon it seems as if such things were bound to happen that way anyhow. Pretty soon we can see only good things instead of God.

About the one who turned back to give thanks to God and offer his song of salvation before the Lord, St. Luke tells us that "he saw that he was healed." He saw more than a change in his physical or social condition. He saw the grace of God at work in the Lord Jesus. He saw the possibility and the reality of a new life under God. He had been restored to soundness of health. The saving power of God had changed not just his circumstances but his whole person. And he returned to give thanks in Christ's presence.

William Hulme, in his book *Dialogue in Despair,* writes:

> There is no dynamic for healing more potent than gratitude. When man prays to God and God accepts him, he enters into God's presence with joy. He shares with his fellowman the good news of his salvation. His praising of God is an expression of his health. (P. 117)

This remarkable insight teaches us that the song of joy in our hearts *is* salvation, *is* soundness of health. Health is not just the absence of suffering or sickness; health is the ability of man to praise God, to make known God's mighty deeds, to share good news with his fellowman.

Health is harmony. That's what we were created for in the beginning. The paradise of Eden, which we can only recall with symbolic pictures, was not simply an existence in which man's environment was in complete balance and in which his physical and psychological makeup remained intact. The joy of man in the beginning was not in his perfect surroundings but in his God. His health was first a harmonious relationship with God and then with the creation around him. And man remained healthy, not as long as he was able to maintain a state of perfection but as he responded to God with the worship of faith and trust and service. Health, then, was peace with God, love for God, responsibility on behalf of God for His creation. The song itself was a sign of health.

One day the singing became silent. Man stopped drawing water from the wells of salvation, from the abundance of God's grace. Instead he turned in upon himself, sought joy in his health. He broke with God. He lost his identity. He became a victim of fear and guilt. Everything got out of balance, even the cells in man's body. Sinful man got sick and died as disease, disorder, and death set in.

It is not necessary to dwell upon the beginnings to see our problem. From our own experience in the present we know something of the disintegrating and destructive forces in life. It doesn't take a Rhodes scholar to know that the world is in a state of disorder. We don't like to hear that the world is dying, that ours is a sick society; we don't like to confess that "there is no health in us." Still the reality of human misery, helplessness, and stupidity cannot be denied. Who is not ready to declare that we need to be saved from poverty and war and disease and universal extinction? Who doesn't want to be saved from himself, from his self-centeredness and even his self-destructiveness?

Our problem is more than what we are afraid might happen or what we might do. Our sin is also what by nature we are incapable of doing, namely, to love and trust God, to worship and serve Him, to express a wholesome relationship with Him through acts of loving service to our neighbor. To be healed for that kind of life, to rise from violence toward others and silence toward God, and to sing a song of thanksgiving—that is our desperate need.

Oh, to sing again, to praise God not only with our lips but with our lives, to know and feel the surge of God's Holy Spirit, to be healthy and whole! That would be salvation. That is how the children of Israel must have felt as they languished in an Egyptian slavery. In that alien land they were no people. They had little incentive to live, much less to praise God. There were no songs—just sighs, a suffering in silence. For how long? Until God showed them that He was still in charge of history, that His promises meant something, that He was not about to create them and make them His own for nothing!

He raised up Moses, who led His people to safety across the Red Sea. Then, as we read in the Book of Exodus, "Moses and the people of Israel sang this song to the Lord, saying, 'I will sing to the Lord, for He has triumphed gloriously; the horse and his rider He has thrown into the sea. The Lord is my strength and my song, and he has become my salvation' " (Exodus 15:1-2a). It was the experience of God's saving power that gave them life and health.

Over the years, especially in time of great distress, the remembrance of God's grace sustained the nation. The Exodus experience was the source of joy and hope expressed in a psalm of the prophet which was formed on the lips of those Israelites who faced captivity a few hundred years later under another nation:

> Behold, God is my salvation;
>> I will trust, and will not be afraid;
> for the Lord God is my strength and
>> my song,
>> and He has become my salvation.
> With joy you will draw water from
>> the wells of salvation. And you will
> say in that day:
>> "Give thanks to the Lord,
>>> call upon His name;
>> make known His deeds among the nations,
>> proclaim that His name is exalted."
>
>>> (Isaiah 12:2-4)

At that point God was still rolling up His sleeves for action. His Word in that situation came through a nation as a Word of promise, even a Word of deliverance. But there was much more to come. According to His agenda of history He would bring healing to the world through a Man, Jesus of Nazareth.

There was no part of man that our Lord failed to heal. He brought wholeness to people's bodies and minds and spirits. Most of all, by means of His cross He turned back the destructive forces of sin and death decisively and convincingly. He won back the family of man, the created order from the Evil One. He gathered us all into the healing relationship of forgiveness, creating a well of salvation from which every believer could draw strength and health for the living of his life.

That is the song of salvation. And that Word is something more than poetic, dreamy words about how we would like things to be, a religious hope or idea. Not this song! The healing of the universe was a direct and personal act of God right here in time and history. Salvation, as the Bible explains it, is a mighty and merciful work of God by which He turns a real, brutal, wretched, and sick episode of history into a saving event. In our Lord's person God carries out His purpose of judging, healing, and renewing the earth.

And that has tremendous consequences for our lives. Wherever we have God's Word and Sacraments we are caught up in God's redeeming action. When we worship we are celebrating with thanksgiving and hope these events by which God has made salvation a reality. We have in the Gospel of Jesus Christ a healing Word which even a world at peace — if that were possible in this age — could not create, and still a healing Word which all the suffering and sickness, the disorder and death we experience in this world could never take from us. We stand in a relationship of forgiveness and integrity with God and with one another. We have been healed at the center of our beings, for God has become our strength and our song and our salvation.

We are therefore able to engage in the noblest activity of man: to eat, drink and be merry, which is to worship and give thanks to God, not simply as an expression for this or that good fortune we have fallen upon, but as an expression of that health and life God has given us in Jesus Christ.

In my experience as a pastor I have found that where people feel they are not worth anything, that they are better off dead, they are saying, in effect, that they aren't worth saving or that they can't be saved. They are mostly in silent despair. When, however, they discover that the God who saved Israel, who raised the Lord Jesus from the dead, has a Word for them that satisfies their hunger and thirst, that gives them a sense of oneness with Him and others, that promises them at last the full victory of Christ their eyes light up. They begin to smile again and sing to God because they have been restored to soundness of health.

Thus we hear the word:

> Give thanks to the Lord,
>   call upon His name;
> make known His deeds among the nations,
> proclaim that His name is exalted.
>
> (Isaiah 12:3)

And so we pray:

> Almighty and immortal God, Giver of life and health: We beseech You to hear our prayers for all Your servants for whom we implore Your mercy, that by Your blessing upon us and upon those who minister to us of Your healing gifts, we may give thanks to You in Your holy church; through Jesus Christ, our Lord. Amen.

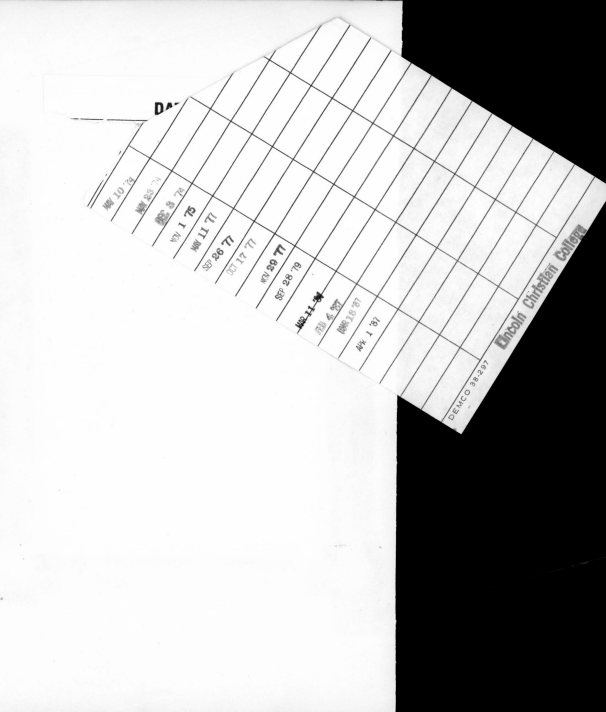